Living Through Loss, Healing Through Jesus

My Story Of Loss And Recovery

Kathy Wright-Key

Copyright © 2023

All Rights Reserved

Dedication

To my children, Nathan and Madi Wright. May you always remember how much I love you and how proud I am to be your mother.

Acknowledgment

I would like to acknowledge the people who supported and encouraged me while writing this book:

I would like to thank my husband- Doug, my children – Nathan and Madison, my sister – Sherri, and my mom- Peggy, for their love and support during the difficulties I have faced and for their encouragement to write this book.

Without your support, I would not have had the strength to finish this book. I want all of you to know how much you mean to me and how much I love you all.

CONTENTS

Dedication	3
Acknowledgment	4
About the Author	7
Prologue	10
Chapter 1	12
Broken Family	12
Chapter 2	20
God's Provision – Church Family	20
Chapter 3	24
Shattered New Beginnings	24
Chapter 4	33
God's Provision – New Friendships	33
Chapter 5	37
Job Loss	37
Chapter 6	46
God's Provision – Encouragement & Confidence	46
Chapter 7	50

Leaving Home Again	50
Chapter 8	60
God's Provision – Renewed Hope	60
Chapter 9	64
Devastating Loss	64
Chapter 10	82
God's Provision – A Closer Walk With Jesus	82
Conclusion	97

About the Author

Hello, my name is Kathy Wright-Key. I am married to my wonderful husband, Doug, and have two children, Nathan and Madison, and four bonus children, Jonathan, Paul, Bradley, and Cameron. I also have two beautiful daughters in love, Ceci and Alex, and three beautiful grandchildren, Liam, Stetson, and Sofia.

I work as an Administrative Assistant for a family business in Dallas and spend my spare time trying to spend as much time as I can with my kids and grandkids, going to movies, crafting and decorating, and working on my second book.

I have experienced many losses throughout my life, but I believe the hardest loss was the loss of my first husband; Mike. It was tragic, unexpected, and devastating. A few years after he passed, I had several friends going through a similar situation and calling me to talk and ask for advice. I felt God leading me to write a book about my experiences so I could share some hope and encouragement with others. This started off as a book specifically for widows, but God had other plans and led me to include additional losses I experienced so it would help not only widows, but many people who have experienced other losses similar to mine.

It took several years to put my thoughts on paper and several tears to complete the book. It was a humbling and healing experience, and I know that God is divinely responsible for allowing me to finish the book and share my story.

I am grateful to my readers and pray that this book will provide healing, comfort, and a fresh perspective on loss and how God is there for us even in our deepest pain.

I look forward to writing many more books and pray you will enjoy reading this book.

Prologue

As I begin writing this book, I am about to celebrate my 50th birthday. While some may look at this number and think I'm old, others will say that I am still young. I believe that I alternate between the two.

For the sake of full disclosure, God has been working on me to write this book for the last 15 years. I have experienced many losses in my life, a recurring theme of this book. I am confident many of you have as well. I pray this book provides a sense of hope, understanding, and the faithfulness of God to each of us.

I do not believe in coincidence; God puts us through many issues in our lives to teach us, strengthen us, or guide us back to Him. I remember telling God through each loss that I needed to have a reason for the loss. I had to later understand I may never know why I experienced each loss on this side of heaven, and beyond that point, it will not matter.

As I share my life experiences, I hope you will gain insight by seeing how the Lord intervened in my life throughout all the hardships my family and I have endured. It was not easy, and I had to remain close to the Lord, even when I received no answers. However, as I look back at each situation and recall the people God sent into my life at just the right time, I can see His handprint on my life. Remember, as you are experiencing difficulties in your life due to loss, Jesus knows why and how He will use these losses as your testimony and to help someone else through a difficult journey. After I realized this, God expressed to me the need for this book.

I would like to thank my husband, Doug. My children – Nathan and Madison, my sister, Sherri, and my mom, Peggy, for their love and support during the difficulties I have faced and for their encouragement to write this book. Know that as I write, I am praying for God's divine peace and comfort for you in your time of loss and sorrow.

Chapter 1

Broken Family

I was three years old when my father left my mother. They had been married for 13 years at the time.

My mother came from a humble background. My grandmother was a simple woman who didn't caution her about the cunning ways of the world. As a result, my mother missed lectures on a lot of important things – including the 'sex' talk.

My parents met in dancing school as teenagers when they became dance partners. They began to date, and without any knowledge or warnings, she got into a sexual relationship with my father. They were both young and did not take any precautions, and unfortunately, my mom became pregnant at 14 years of age.

Although my father had no intention of marrying my mother, my paternal grandmother insisted he marry her. He was just a kid himself and was reluctant, but in the end, he gave in to his mother's constant attempts. Back then, having children out of wedlock was heavily frowned upon. So, she made him do what she deemed was the right thing. My parents married at the justice of the peace in their hometown of Haverhill, Massachusetts.

During their marriage, my mom gave birth to five children: two girls and three boys. Two of my brothers died shortly after they were born. There was a large gap between myself and my siblings. When I was born, my sister was ten years older, and my brother was seven years older.

Both my parents had to quit high school because of their new lives and responsibilities. Society wasn't kind to unmarried couples, so they had no other option but to leave their education halfway through. Due to her age and lack of education, her mom became a homemaker. Her job was to look after her children and the house. As a result, my father was the sole breadwinner of the house. We lived in an apartment on the second floor above two older ladies who were kind to my mom and helped her many times. My father was the only one who drove, so my mom and us kids had to walk wherever we needed to go if my dad was not at home.

Seeing that I was only three when my dad left, I do not recall much of him in our home. I am unsure if my brain retracted those memories for my well-being or if it was something else. After my dad left, my mother had to find a job with little to no skill set. My sister was a teenager, and my brother was a preteen when my father left. This was extremely difficult for them since they had spent so much time with him.

When my father left my mom, he moved in with another woman. My sister, my brother, and I would go to their house for visits. Upon returning home from visiting my dad, my mother would drill my older sister and brother for information. Eventually, she stopped letting me go. She wanted to shelter me from seeing my father living with another woman.

My siblings still wanted to go, so they were allowed to. With the passage of time, my father stopped fighting for visitation rights to see me. I never knew any better since I was so little; it wouldn't trigger feelings of loss until I was older. A few years later, my father remarried, and they moved to California and soon after to Texas. My siblings did not see him much after that.

My grandparents helped my mom financially for as long as they could. We moved into a smaller apartment but were barely getting by financially. My mom was on welfare and devastated as she did not have a high school diploma or work experience. My mom went back to get her GED and found a childcare job.

My mom was in extreme shock, depression, and denial. She was in no emotional condition to do anything at all. As a result, my sister took over and became the 'mother' of our family. She started working at the age of 15 to help us with the money. My mom didn't realize it but being the eldest put a great amount of pressure on my sister.

Of the few memories I recall of my childhood, I remember not knowing we were poor. Life as we lived it was all I knew. Nowhere in my memories was I taught the concept of rich and poor.

I remember being the mascot for my sister's high school drill team. My grandmother made me a uniform that matched their school colors. I loved marching with them at the football games and Christmas parades. The parades would always end near a McDonald's. One of my sister's guy friends treated me like a little sister. He would always treat me to a Happy Meal at the end of the parade, and I would get to hang out with all the drill team and my sister's friends.

I felt terrible for my brother. My sister had many friends from school, and they were always over. She was dating and had people in her life to get her mind off my dad leaving. My poor brother felt so lonely and insecure. He lived in a house full of women, and he felt as though he was unloved and unwelcome. He went back and forth to my father's, to gain his love and attention; however, he was met by my uncaring stepmother and her girls. He eventually gave up going to my father's house. He craved a relationship with his father but, unfortunately, never received one.

A few years after my father left, a brand-new low-income housing development was opening. My mom decided to apply since the money was tight, and we qualified! These apartments and townhomes had a pool and playgrounds and were within walking distance of the grocery store and Kmart. We were given a three-bedroom townhouse.

The apartment complex was very nice. We had great neighbors, and we were able to play in the neighborhood. My mom made friends with the lady next door, and she was a hairdresser who did my mom's hair at a discounted rate. Since my grandparents were aging and needing additional assistance, they decided to move into the senior apartments in the same complex, so we were all close together. This made seeing them and helping them much easier for her.

We did not have a washer and dryer in the apartment and would have to go to the laundromat. I remember in the winter; mom would load up our baskets of laundry with me on a sled. My sister's boyfriend would pull me down the hill to the laundromat! My sister and her boyfriend didn't mind this chore, as they got to spend more time together.

I, too, loved going to the laundromat. They had carts on wheels that customers would use to empty the clothes out of the washer to move to the dryers. My brother would load me in the cart, and we would race around the laundry mat at least until we got caught! They also had the Ms. Pac-Man video game I loved. Mom would always let me get a Tab soda which was another reason why I loved going there.

My mom was so depressed she had no energy to think about feeding us healthy meals. Despite the lack of money, she always found a way to get us subs, McDonald's, and other unhealthy foods. There was a store up the street from our apartment that allowed us to have a charge account. We would go to this store and get candy, soda, or whatever else we could find.

When we went to the grocery store, my siblings would 'hide' junk food in the cart. Mom wouldn't see it until we got to the register. They would just laugh and act like they had no idea how the food got in the cart.

Once my sister graduated high school, she married her high school sweetheart at 18. After living in Massachusetts for a year, she and her husband decided to move to Texas to be near my father and try to restore their relationship.

We were sad to see our sister leave. She was the responsible adult who took care of us. Not only that, but she had a lot of friends. They were in our house so frequently that they were all a part of the family. With her gone, all of that came to an end.

My mom was especially sad when my sister relocated. However, she knew that it was time for her to step up and take charge. Soon, she found a better-paying job at a church in Salem, NH.

This church had a daycare, as well as a Christian school. My brother and I could attend for free since my mom worked at the church. My brother was now a teenager, and I was barely a preteen. My brother stayed at the school for a year but never felt he fit in. He did not make many friends. At the age of seventeen, he joined the Navy. This left mom and me alone. This was the point where I began feeling the impact of my mom's divorce. I had always had my sibling at home to provide company and entertainment. In some ways, they sheltered me. It became hard now that they were both gone.

My mom and I had to move into a two-bedroom apartment since the townhouse were too large for just the two of us. Our new neighbor was a single woman, and my mom and I became instant friends.

With the departure of my siblings, my mom began dating more regularly. It was tough for me as I was already lonely, and now, I would have to go to my grandparents' apartment with no one to play with.

My grandmother pitied me and did her best to cheer me up. She would sew new dresses for my dolls to make me happy. I wasn't that grateful back then, but looking back, I sincerely wish I had appreciated all the time I had with my grandparents.

If it hadn't been for my grandmother, I'm not sure how my mom would have made it. She was her encouragement, counselor, and help in all her sorrow and distress. To be honest, my grandmother was the source of light in my suddenly lonely and dark life, too.

When I turned ten, my grandmother had a severe stroke. She could no longer take care of herself or her husband. My mom had to make the difficult decision to put them in a nursing home.

I remember I hated going to visit as my grandmother was not able to speak anymore; she could only mumble. I would watch as she cried, trying to talk with us. My grandfather begged my mom not to leave him there. He was crippled, and there was no way my mom could care for him. My grandfather passed away about six months after moving to the nursing home. My grandmother held on for another year.

Things only got harder with their passing away. I noticed how much more stressed mom became. She had lost her husband, children, and parents in the span of years. She was constantly worrying about money. She was also lonely and afraid, struggling to make ends meet. I knew that she just wanted to settle with someone who would take care of her. With each passing day, worry, and stress seemed to eat her away.

Chapter 2

God's Provision – Church Family

Although my mom was a single parent of three, the Lord made sure we always had people who watched out and were there for us. As I got older, I became very active in my church and youth group. It can be said that our church adopted my mom and me.

We were there every time the doors were open, and I felt like everyone was my extended family. My teachers at the Christian school became like aunts and uncles to me. Without them in my life, I know it would have been a very lonely existence for both of us. They brought back a lot of laughter and fulfillment as they knew my loneliness. They always brought me back to how the Lord loves the lonely and brokenhearted. I knew each of them had my back and was assisting my mom with my upbringing.

"The LORD is close to the brokenhearted and saves those who are crushed in spirit."
Psalms 34:18

Even when my mom was at the end of her rope, God always provided for us. He never lets His people down. I don't know how many times she would be worried or concerned over something, and God would show up for us. He would bestow His blessings upon us and leave us in awe of the way He worked things out for His loved ones.

There was this one time when she wasn't sure how she would get me new clothes and pay for them. Out of the blue, a lady from our church offered to sew all my clothes for me. We were so grateful that we didn't think there was more to it. But there was! Some ladies dropped off brand-new clothes for me to have and wear.

There were also times when our resources were stretched thin, and we'd worry about not having anything to eat. Then, through His people, God would show up for us. Many times, people from our church would randomly appear at our apartment. They would come bearing food or carrying bags full of groceries for us.

Looking back, I can see that God *always* provided for us. I know He did this because my mom always taught me that even if you cannot afford to tithe, make sure you do. God always blessed us abundantly because my mom feared the Lord and was faithful to Him.

"For He will command His angels concerning you to guard you in all your ways. On their hands, they will bear you up, lest you strike your foot against a stone."
Psalm 91:11-12

The hardest part about being the only child at home with a single mom was that I had no one to play with. One of my best friends from church would often invite me over to her house. She had six siblings, and they were a lot of fun. I remember being jealous that she had both of her parents and all her siblings around. I loved spending time with her and her family.

Growing up, I would invite her to our apartment on Sundays after church. This became a frequent habit, and mom would always take us out to this special steakhouse at the mall. It was a special place, and I loved their food. I still remember my order: I always got the hamburger, steak fries, and chocolate pudding! My friend enjoyed the food as well, and we had a lot of fun. But she really loved the peace and quiet my house had to offer, as opposed to her house.

As I began junior high, I had a difficult time as all of my friends at school were involved in dancing school or other fun extracurricular activities. The problem with having a good time and enjoying yourself is that it does not come cheap. My mom could not afford to do those things for me.

Again, I had teachers and church people who would encourage me and help me to remember all that God had done for me. This is how I learned the difference between wants and needs. I believe God wanted me to know that even though I could not have everything I wanted, I had all I needed.

"But my God shall supply all your needs according to his riches in glory by Christ Jesus."
Philippians 4:19

In December of 1984, my eighth-grade year, I received the best surprise in my life. It was totally unexpected.

I had a lead role in my school Christmas play, and at the end, I was looking for my mom and saw my sister and brother-in-law in the audience! They had moved back home! I was so excited to see them. My brother had also come back from the military around the same time.

I was on cloud nine and felt like our family was finally together, restored.

Chapter 3

Shattered New Beginnings

Due to the fact that my siblings moved away after my grandparents' death, my mom and I got extremely close with one another. After all, we only had each other.

Therefore, I had a hard time whenever she would go on dates. I spent a lot of time alone at the apartment when she would go out. It was difficult, but I knew my mom deserved happiness, so I didn't complain.

My sister and brother-in-law moved to Framingham, Massachusetts, when they returned since my brother-in-law found a job there. My brother was close to my sister and her husband, so he also decided to move there as well.

My sister had me visit on occasional weekends and encouraged me to begin talking with my father over the phone. I had not seen or spoken with him since he left when I was four. This was somewhat of a rollercoaster of feelings for me: it was exciting and scary at the same time. It opened up a whole world of possibilities for me. But it was a door that had been shut for a long time, and I worried about how opening that door would unfold.

Although my siblings moved about 40 minutes from where we lived, I spent a lot of time with them on the weekends. I looked forward to weekends once they moved back. It felt great to be reunited with my family once again.

One day, we were at my sister's house when she encouraged me to speak to my father. We hadn't been in contact since I was a little girl, but I felt convinced after talking to my sister. My father and I started speaking over the phone from that point forward. After several calls, he invited me to go to Texas over the summer to visit him. I was excited, and I wanted to go, so I agreed.

I had been informed at the end of my 8th-grade year that the school I had been attending was not going to offer high school classes due to a lack of admission. This meant I would have to begin public school, and I was very nervous and anxious. I had not been to a public school since I was in second grade, and I would have to go to one in the town where we lived. I did not have any friends in my hometown since we spent all our time in New Hampshire at church and school. I thought that going away for a few weeks would help me work off the stress.

Eventually, I decided it was time to tell mom everything. I confessed that I had been in touch with him and also told her that he had invited me and I had accepted. Mom didn't really like it. Nor was she particularly excited about the aspect of us being so far apart from one another for such a long time. But she understood that it was important to me, so she agreed to let me go.

As the trip came closer, I experienced a whirlwind of emotions. I was happy and excited but also worried about how the visit would pan out. I was flooded with a thousand questions and what-ifs.

What was my dad really like? What if his personality in real life didn't match his personality over the phone? Would he like me? Would he say that he was proud of me? What if my dad didn't like me the way I was?

What would I feel when I would see him? Would the visit be pleasant? Would the two of us get along and pretend that we hadn't been complete strangers for years? Would it be awkward or uncomfortable? Would we address the discomfort?

I didn't know the answer to any of these questions. But I desperately needed these answers. I knew that there was only one way to find it. Time seemed to fly, and summer came soon enough. I left on a plane to Wichita Falls, TX, to see my dad in June 1985.

Luckily, after meeting him, I realized that my fears were groundless. My father was very excited to see me; it was fun being with him. I was surprised the first time I saw him, taken aback by just how much the two of us looked alike.

We had a short drive to his house in Burkburnett since it was only 15 minutes away. He had planned a lot of fun activities for us to do while I was there. My dad and stepmother had adopted a newborn baby in 1981, and this was the first time I had seen him. At the time of my visit, my stepmother seemed pleasant and acted happy that I was there. I had a difficult time understanding why my siblings had a difficult time getting along with her; she seemed quite pleasant.

A few weeks after coming to visit my dad, he asked if I would like to stay for the summer. I quickly agreed since I was having so much fun there. So, a few weeks turned into a longer trip.

About a month into my stay, he asked me if I wanted to live with him and my stepmother. I had mixed emotions about this. On the one hand, I really enjoyed my time here. On the flip side, I knew that my mom was back home, all alone. I felt bad for leaving her behind, and I didn't know how she'd feel if I extended my stay again. However, my dad kept pressing the issue, and I eventually decided to stay. After all, we had spent 14 years apart. It felt like the right thing to do.

Once I decided to stay, I spoke with my dad about getting involved in a church since I had been attending church at an early age. My father and stepmother did not go to church, but he was happy to go to church with me. Although my stepmother decided not to attend, as she was not an active church participant, he took my stepbrother as well.

After searching for a church, we chose the First Baptist Church (FBC) of Burkburnett, TX. I will not forget the first time I attended Sunday school at FBC; people in Texas are friendly, but small towns are not very welcoming to new people. Everyone acted friendly, but no one rushed over to talk to me. It was strange and not at all what I had been accustomed to.

A few girls who were juniors in high school decided to reach out and welcome me. Debbie was one of the girls who went out of her way to make me feel at home. She was an extreme extrovert, and seeing a very shy Yankee girl who did not trust strangers sparked something within her; she did everything she could to 'break' me out of my shell. We soon became great friends, and she helped me get to know people during my first summer in Texas.

As summer came to an end, it was time to begin my freshman year at Burkburnett High School. Having attended a private school during my elementary and junior high years, beginning a public school in a new town was very intimidating. This was a tough transition for me, but I must credit Debbie for helping me survive new experiences and partially breaking me out of my shyness. I met two incredibly good friends, and my transition to the new school went well.

Debbie was great at helping me learn my way around the school and introduced me to many new friends. I spent many Friday nights at Debbie's house with her family, who welcomed me like another daughter. She had three older brothers who had already left home and one younger brother who was a year younger than me. A few times, she tried to set us up as a couple, but I quickly informed her, "I was not interested." As far as I was concerned, he was an eighth grader and was not my type.

After a few months of living with my dad and stepmom, things began to unravel. The newness wore off, and my stepmother determined she was not my biggest fan. That's when things started to go downhill. Or perhaps, they had been like that for a while, and I didn't exactly notice it?

I did not get to speak to my mom or siblings very often. My grades in the first semester were not good. Having attended a Christian school making straight A's, the school put me in advanced placement classes, and it was much harder than private school had been. I was terribly upset, and a few months into the school year, I asked my dad to let me return to Massachusetts.

My dad convinced me to stay; however, my stepmother decided she did not like me after that. She told me several times that she couldn't stand me, and I reminded her of my mother. She looked for any way possible to get me in trouble with my dad. She often lied about things I did just so I would get grounded. They gave me excessive chores, and I was miserable trying to balance all of it while also listening to the bitterness that seemed to seep out of my stepmother's heart so easily.

It was as though my bubble had suddenly burst, and now I was trapped in darkness. The only positive things I had were attending school to see my friends and attending church functions. My friends and church were helpful in keeping my mind off my problems at home. It was the only bright part that remained in my life.

After the end of the first semester, my dad was furious. My grades were poor, and he was upset. He laid out new rules for me: I was required to stay in my room and do homework for at least two hours each day until my grades improved.

I knew that the problem was something else and that there was another way to fix it. I met with the counselor, and a lot of things were resolved after that meeting. I changed some of my classes, which helped a great deal. My grades improved, and things calmed down at home for a while.

My dad tried so hard to keep the peace at home. He knew how stressed my stepmother made me, but I think he felt helpless. He was afraid to lose his marriage due to arguments over his daughter. It was a tough first year, but I was able to get through it somehow.

As soon as the summer of 1986 began, I continued attending several church events. Debbie and I spent time together almost every weekend. I loved going to her house to get away from the tension at home.

I was sad to see summer go by so quickly. Debbie was beginning her senior year, and I was only a sophomore. I began to wonder how I would make it once she graduated. Debbie continued taking me places and introducing me to people, trying to break me out of my shyness. I got embarrassed easily, and she loved it. I can recall that she was always on the hunt, looking for guys with whom she could set me up. It was crazy, but we always had a great time. I made more friends in my sophomore year and finally had a good variety of both church and school friends.

My sophomore year ended quickly, and Debbie graduated. I wanted to spend as much time as possible with her during her last semester of high school. About a week before Debbie's graduation, my dad discovered he was being laid off from his job. Thus began his plans to move to Alabama.

I had no interest in going there. My world was in Texas now. I had no intention of leaving all that behind, simply to put up with the ugly home environment and my stepmother's tantrums, so I refused. Debbie's parents even offered me to stay with them till I finished high school, but my dad didn't agree. He was against the idea, and it led to several arguments.

Eventually, my dad told me that I was going to go to Massachusetts for a visit to see my mom and siblings. I had no idea that he was sending me back home, and he had no intention of calling me back or moving me to Alabama with the rest of his family.

In 1987, I returned home to Massachusetts on vacation, except it *wasn't*.

Chapter 4

God's Provision – New Friendships

It was so exciting when I went to Texas to visit my father. He and my stepmother took me shopping, to Six Flags and several new places. I received the attention I had not received from my mom since she started dating, and I felt important again. Not that my mom meant to ignore me. I was just fourteen and was unable to understand what she needed.

When my father asked me if I wanted to live with him, I had no idea what was happening at home with my mom. She seemed emotional every time I spoke with her, but I knew she was missing me. Although I was concerned about my mom, I felt like she would be okay since she had her boyfriend, and I did not want to go to the high school I was scheduled to attend. I did not know anyone, and I was deathly afraid. I was a very quiet, introverted girl and was terrified. I called my mom to ask if I could stay in Texas, and she began crying. She told me I could if that was what I wanted. I told her it was. Little did I realize that my mom would have to have a hysterectomy. No one told me until years later.

God knew that I needed to have the security of friends and church to be able to handle all that was happening with the tension in my family. I was very involved in our church youth group, which would become my saving grace. I went to church camps in the summer, was in the youth choir at church, and participated in any activity I could. I made great friends and spent time with them as often as my dad would allow.

God truly protected me and knew that I would need to be strong to handle everything happening at home. Being around Debbie and her family gave me confidence in myself as a person.

"Many will say they are loyal friends, but who can find one who is truly reliable?"
Proverbs 20:6

I had been highly sheltered by my mother and lacked confidence when trying to meet someone new. All I had known my entire life was the people from my small church in New Hampshire. After being around Debbie, I gained more confidence in who I was and gained the courage to get out of my "comfort zone" and meet new people.

Debbie was always trying to set me up with people. I had never had a boyfriend, and this was a big learning experience. She was in the high school band, knew a lot of people, and constantly introduced me to guys she thought I would like, and that's how I met my first boyfriend. Since I was dating someone in the band and most of my friends were also in the band, we spent time together at football games and began to socialize more.

Hanging out with Debbie and some other friends taught me the value of close relationships.

"Therefore, encourage one another and build one another up, just as you are doing."
1 Thessalonians 5:11

She was more than a friend; she was like a sister. I never understood how much this two-year experience would impact my future. Debbie often invited me to her house to spend the night. She was fully aware of what was happening in my life and wanted to do what she could to help.

I recall my dad giving me a watch on my sixteenth birthday. I was so disheartened as my mom would have thrown me a huge party. To me, this was a historic event! Dad did not believe in birthday parties, and I was crushed; however, my friends planned a surprise party, which was wonderful. I felt more at home at my friend's house than I did at my own.

God provided great friends, church activities, great youth ministers, and my friends' parents who invested in my life.

Chapter 5

Job Loss

Once I arrived in Massachusetts, I stayed at my sister and brother-in-law's apartment. There, I found out that my dad had intentionally sent me home. He knew how much his wife hated me and thought I would be better off moving back to Massachusetts. My mom was engaged, and it was not comfortable for me to live with her. My sister and brother-in-law gave me the option of living with them to finish high school, and I accepted.

After moving home, I was able to work on my relationship with my brother and restore it. The seven-year age difference seemed to dissipate as I was now older. He was at my sister's house often, and we had some great times catching up. I was happy that we were growing closer.

I had to find a job since my sister could not afford to pay for all my expenses and support me. I found a job at a local pizza place and had to walk to work since I did not own a car. I met a lot of great people and made friends quickly. I enjoyed working there and quickly befriended a guy who I worked with.

He was sweet and gave me rides home so I did not have to walk. He wanted to date me, but I was afraid of losing our friendship and kept putting him off. Toward the middle of my first summer, my sister advised we needed to find a new place to live since she was pregnant. I was now living with them, sleeping on their couch since they only had a one-bedroom apartment. My friend's parents had an apartment in their house above their apartment. He told me about it, and after my sister and brother-in-law saw it, they decided it would be perfect. We moved right before I began my junior year of high school.

Now that I was living above my friend, he kept insisting we at least go on a date and see what happened. I agreed, and we began dating. He truly helped me by being one of my closest friends, and we dated throughout my junior year. We went to prom together, and I began to think we would end up getting married. We would discuss it often. He was two years older than me and was not planning to attend a four-year university.

During the summer, my sister noticed that we were getting close, and she suggested I be careful not to plan to marry the first guy I dated since moving back. She thought it would be a good idea for me to date other people and not get too serious with anyone my age. I broke up with him and felt terrible about it. It was so awkward living above him and his family now that we weren't together anymore. I started my senior year without a boyfriend, but I made more friends. I decided to take business classes since I planned to work full-time after graduation.

  I had wonderful teachers who invested in me, knowing I lived with my sister and did not have parents assisting me in college plans. These teachers helped me get an interview for a part-time job at a computer company right up the street from the school. After I got the job, I could go to school in the mornings and then work in the afternoon. This provided me with great experience in the business world. I was an assistant to the secretary, and she taught me a great deal about clerical duties and working as a team.

  I flourished in the business classes at my school. My accounting teacher asked me to be her assistant managing the books for the school bank and store. I made it into Business Professionals of America. I won the first competition and made it to the Nationals, which ironically were in Dallas, TX. I could not afford the trip, but my work sponsored my way. The trip was in the spring, and I was super excited.

  Towards the middle of my senior year, the counselor called me in to discuss college. I explained that I had not considered a college career and would pursue a full-time job after graduation; since my options for attending college were not relayed to me, I could have been eligible to receive grants and possibly a free education.

In the early spring, one of my good friends introduced me to a new guy at school. I was instantly attracted as he was tall, dark, and handsome. I was in love, or so I thought. He was so sweet and came from a wonderful family.

Business Professionals of America was a few weeks after we met, and I did not want to go. I wanted to spend as much time with him as possible as I knew he was going to college, but I was not. We spent a lot of time talking over the phone, and although I was not supposed to make any phone calls while I was in Texas, I called him from the hotel. I did not win the competition, but I was not concerned. I was infatuated with this guy. I connected with my friend Debbie while I was in Dallas. She had moved to Dallas to go to a secretarial school and wasn't far from the hotel I was staying at. She came to see me, and we had a great time reconnecting.

Once I came back from the competition in Texas, time seemed to fly. Before I knew it, the school year was over. A few weeks before graduation, my sister announced that she was moving, and I needed to find a place to live. I was scared and not sure what I was going to do. I spoke with my friends and my teachers to get some advice. I knew I would have to work full-time to support myself and would have to find a place to live. I only had a few weeks to figure things out since my sister had to move by the end of May. Through the assistance of some of my high school teachers, I was able to find a full-time job at AT&T. I finished my classes a few weeks before graduation and was asked to begin working at my new job at AT&T.

While my friends were enjoying their last summer before college, I was going to work full-time. One of my close friends told me she spoke with her parents, and I could live with them through the summer while searching for a place to call my own. I was so excited about my upcoming prom and graduation that the reality of the situation hadn't set in. I knew my boyfriend was heading to college in a few short months, and I wanted to see him as much as possible. I was devastated that my boyfriend and I had to break up once the summer ended. I knew I needed to find a place to live since my living situation was temporary, and I eventually rented a room from a sweet lady in Framingham.

Since I was working full time and my friends had all left for college, I was without anyone to hang out with. During this time, my brother and I began hanging out more. I noticed he was nervous most of the time. He and his girlfriend had broken up, and he was extremely depressed.

However, being eighteen, I was unaware of what he was going through. I mentioned this to my sister. She was now living in New Hampshire, and he was at her home often, and she noticed it as well. Unfortunately, my mom was newly married and did not know how to deal with my brother's issues. My sister was stressed, not knowing what to do to help my brother.

He was in and out of the VA hospitals many times and started to walk the streets. We found out he had schizophrenia and was mentally unable to stay in one place for any length of time. He thought people were following him, and he was terrified all the time. It was so sad to watch, and no one in my family knew what to do. Neither of my parents wanted to handle the situation. With me being so young, my poor sister had to take a lot of the responsibility of helping him.

While working for AT&T, I moved offices three times due to being a part of a secretarial pool. I made many great friends at work, and they included me in activities outside the office, although I was a lot younger than most of them. A few of the guys I worked with asked me out on dates, and some friends set me up with some guys they knew. I never found anyone whom I was truly interested in pursuing a long-term relationship with. I really missed my high school boyfriend, and we did get together one time after he went to college, but he had no interest in forming a relationship again as he was far away and dating other girls.

About a year after graduating high school, I attempted to restore my relationship with my mom. I started going to visit her more often, and we began talking more. After dating her boyfriend for five years, he asked her to marry him. She wanted a large wedding since she had never had that the first time.

My mom asked me to be at her wedding as her maid of honor. She planned her wedding for the fall of 1990. Once she got married, she became very busy as they decided to build a home. The relationship between my siblings, myself, and my mom was very strained due to everything that happened over the years. I was hoping we could all be close again. Although she invested everything in her new husband, I think she did so as she felt very alone. I was happy for her but sad that our family dynamic was so strained.

Soon after my mother remarried, my brother decided that he was a headache to everyone, and he would move to Lynchburg, VA, and attend Liberty University. It had been his dream forever, and he was going to figure out how to do it. He ended up moving, against our better judgment, and he became friends with the pastor's son at Thomas Road Baptist Church in Lynchburg. He was able to obtain a scholarship to attend college, and he had a difficult time.

Due to having been given so many different antipyschotic medications for his schizophrenia and getting on and off them, he developed dystonia, a painful condition affecting the nerves in the neck and face. This caused him to suffer great pain, and he often had to hold his neck to keep his head up. It also caused him to make weird faces. The kids at the college did not understand and made fun of him. He was so upset, and it was an extremely sad situation. None of us knew how to help him.

Due to his disease, he constantly questioned his salvation, and he went to talk to the pastor often. The pastor and his son were so wonderful to him, and we were at least comforted that they were there for him. My sister tried to get him to move back to Massachusetts, but he refused.

In the spring of 1991, my supervisor called me in and explained that my office was declaring a layoff and I would be losing my job. She suggested I look at other AT&T locations. I was still in close contact with my friend Debbie in Texas. Many times, over the two years I had been back in Massachusetts, I called her home phone, and her younger brother Mike answered. Since Debbie was not home, we began conversing and catching up on life. After getting this devastating news of losing my job, I called Debbie, and she suggested I come to work in Texas and live with her. With my boss's help, I scheduled an interview with AT&T in Las Colinas, TX, in May of 1991. I flew to Texas a few weeks later, interviewed with AT&T, and visited with Debbie and Mike. It was a great time visiting, and Mike and I hit it off. After returning home, we continued to talk via phone. We decided we would begin dating if I got the job and moved to Texas. Since he was in college at West TX University (now TX

A&M) in Canyon, TX, we would see each other on the weekends. Flights were reasonable, and we had figured out all the details. It was only a two-hour flight from Dallas to Amarillo, and we decided we could alternate flying to see each other on the weekends. I was waiting to hear back from the AT&T office in Dallas, and about a week after I returned home, I received a call offering me the position.

      My mom and I had worked hard to restore a relationship, but I still felt alone. She was devastated when I explained that I had lost my job and needed to figure out what to do. I explained that I had gotten a job in Texas and that I was going to live with Debbie. She also knew that I wanted to begin a dating relationship with Mike. She cried a lot when she realized I was leaving again, this time for good. It was hard to leave her as we had just started restoring our relationship, but I knew I needed a fresh start.

Chapter 6

God's Provision – Encouragement & Confidence

God knew what He was doing, putting me in classes where teachers knew I did not have the typical family life. They not only tried to help me as much as possible, but they also invested in my future. I was allowed to learn as much as possible about business skills. And through clubs and working for my teacher, I was able to learn accounting.

Not only did this help prepare me for working, but it also helped me mature and be ready to stand on my own when I moved out of my sister's house.

I met two friends who helped me through so many life issues during my last two years in high school. They were there when I needed someone to talk to, and their families "adopted" me as one of the kids and were there for me as well.

"A friend loves at all times, and a brother is born for a time of adversity."

Proverbs 17:17

My friends never gave up on me. One of them even went out of her way to consistently write encouraging letters to keep me encouraged. Also, she constantly reminded me of God's love during that time when I didn't go to church.

I wish I had realized sooner that God was always there for me. When relationships failed, I continually hit rock bottom, and when I couldn't feel my worth; I wish I knew God was there all along. However, I had convinced myself that I was alone without a normal family life.

Subconsciously, I looked for love in all the wrong places. I dated guys I knew were not good for me, and when those relationships didn't work, I would blame myself and convince myself that I was meant to be alone.

If only I understood He had a greater plan. Thankfully, I had good friends to keep me in check, and God broke the relationships off to take care of me. God was already preparing my future husband and me to be ready to get to know each other better.

"For I know the plans I have for you," declares the Lord, *"plans to prosper you and not to harm you, plans to give you hope and a future."*

Jeremiah 29:11

I would never have started talking with Mike if I had not lost my job and begun speaking to Debbie about finding a job in Texas. God had introduced us so many years before, and I never thought we would ever date later in life. God knew we both had a lot of growing up to do to be ready to date each other.

God had already known that I would lose my job by allowing me to have a friend in Texas who would be there for me to help. He allowed me to have two years of experience, learning all I could at the computer company I worked for in high school and another two years of experience working for a major corporation. The skills I learned helped me to find new jobs even though I did not have a college degree.

God also knew it would take great courage and confidence to take care of myself to move two thousand miles away from my family. So, he gave me the confidence to continue my journey in Texas even when I had lost a job before arriving.

I was able to develop a work ethic while living with my sister, as I had to take care of my expenses. Almost instantly, I realized I would need a good job to pay my bills and support myself. Thankfully, God continually brought job opportunities for me, so I had enough money to meet my needs.

God had prepared Mike with the maturity of a stable family to provide me the comfort and security I longed for in a boyfriend. God knew that I would need a strong person to handle all my craziness. He understood what I had been through and knew what I wanted before I even knew for myself.

I needed stability. I wanted my presence to be acknowledged. I yearned to feel loved, supported, and valued. My life had shown me enough instability from being tossed around between my mom, dad, and sister, switching from one guy to another, and losing one friend to looking for another. I had seen enough.

I had always heard that God prepares the right person for you at the right time, but I didn't believe it until I met Mike. I had never met someone like him. Not only was he able to handle all my craziness, but most importantly, he was good at making me feel safe. And when things turned south, he would remind me everything would be okay. And somehow, I began to believe it. Finally, I truly started believing everything would be okay.

Chapter 7

Leaving Home Again

In June 1991, I left Massachusetts with everything I owned in my small car and headed to Texas, which consisted of about $500 and my clothes. My mind, at that moment, was on the butterflies I had in my stomach. I remember looking back one last time at the empty apartment I used to call my home. I remember absorbing everything in sight on the drive to the airport. This place was all I had known, except for the two years I had in Texas, and I was terrified.

Mike was there for me throughout. He had offered to fly up and drive to Texas with me since I was anxious about driving across the country alone. It was a long drive, and to say it was scary would be an understatement. I spent the whole drive constantly worrying about how I would adjust to being back in Texas alone.

To add salt to my wounds, I received a call from my new supervisor at AT&T informing me that he could no longer hire me as they had also declared a layoff. We had just made it to Missouri, and I was about a day's drive from reaching Texas. Now, I had no idea what I was going to do.

I called Debbie, and she still wanted me to come. She said that she would continue to help me find another job. I called my mom, and she wanted me to come home. I knew I did not have a job or a place to stay in Massachusetts, so I continued my trip to Texas. After discussing my options, Mike encouraged me to move to Canyon, where he was attending college, so we could date and see where the relationship took us. He offered to let me stay with him and his roommate until I could figure out what I wanted to do.

A week after I arrived, Mike's parents informed him they were coming for a visit. Mike's family had no idea I had moved to Texas, let alone was dating their son. Mike panicked, and I told him we needed to tell them. He agreed, and we decided to tell his parents when they came to visit.

When they came to visit, they were shocked to see me. They were happy when we explained why I was there and informed them we were dating. However, they were concerned that Mike would not finish college if the relationship turned serious. At the time, I felt they did not want us to date.

A few weeks later, I found a job working for a cell phone company in Amarillo. It wasn't the best job, nor did it pay very well, but it gave me enough money to get my own apartment and stay near Mike.

We dated all summer and knew we wanted to get married. We decided he would continue to go to college and work part-time. In August 1989, Mike asked me to go to dinner and had the waiter bring my diamond ring on the tray, suggesting I might want dessert. He had my ring on a dessert platter and asked me to marry him. We had no idea where we would get married or how we would even pay for a wedding, but we knew we were in love and wanted to get married.

My family had mixed emotions.

Mike had called my dad to ask his permission to marry me. He agreed; however, due to the rocky relationship between my stepmother and me and the distance, he explained that he couldn't attend the wedding.

My mom thought I would move home one day, and now that I was getting engaged, I would remain in Texas. My mom and I had become closer over the last few years, and this was difficult for her. However, after I moved home to Massachusetts, she was engaged to get married, and our relationship was not as close.

My sister was extremely excited and wanted us to get married in New Hampshire. But after we discussed costs, we realized that it was unlikely that it would happen.

I will never forget the day we went to tell Mike's parents. May I say they were less than pleased? They were not upset that we wanted to get married; they were upset that Mike had not finished his education. We explained that he planned to continue attending school even after we married. They strongly advised that we would be on our own. They loved us but were not sure we were doing the right thing.

Mike and I attempted to plan the wedding; however, a college student working a part-time job, and my small salary did not allow for a large wedding. In fact, we found a Bed and Breakfast called the "Hudspeth House" in Canyon, TX, to have our wedding. We decided we did not want to wait a year, so we announced we were getting married on November 9th, 1991, a few months after we got engaged.

Mike's sister, Debbie, was happy but disappointed, as well. She wanted me to move to Dallas and be her roommate. Mike's brothers did not know what to think since they barely knew me. As far as they knew, I was Debbie's best friend and had just moved back to Texas. My mom was happy but sad, as she knew now that I was marrying a Texan, the odds of me moving back to Massachusetts were slim. My sister was thrilled, but she was also sad I was not returning.

We planned a small, intimate wedding, and even though I wanted my family to come, I also understood the expense of flying to Texas for a few days to see me leave on my honeymoon was too much for them.

Seeing how upset I was that my parents would not be able to come and not have my father walk me down the aisle, Mike's father offered to walk me down the aisle. I was thankful for his offer and happily accepted it. Debbie was my maid of honor, and Mike's best friend was his best man.

On November 9th, 1991, we were pronounced: *Mr. and Mrs. Michael Wright.*

The day of the wedding was a beautiful fall day. We had about twenty-five people, and it was simple and cozy. The fireplace was lit in the background as we exchanged our vows with each other, and we were elated. I was happy and ready to begin our new life as husband and wife.

We went to Dallas for our honeymoon. One of the girls I worked with paid for us to stay in a small hotel in Dallas. We stayed for a few days and were bored. Mike spoke to his parents, and they had a timeshare in Oklahoma and said we could stay there for a few days.

Once we returned from our honeymoon, Mike began working full-time at Walmart, and I continued working full-time at the cell phone company. Mike tried to continue his studies but struggled to juggle working full-time and trying to continue full-time studies. Thus, he decided to quit school, and we took on a paper route at 3:00 am each morning to help support us.

We both went through several jobs and often moved to find the "dream job" we thought existed. Finally, after a few years of moving around and different jobs, we moved back to his hometown, Burkburnett, TX, and lived with his parents. I worked as a temporary worker for a local business during this time, and Mike had two part-time jobs.

We knew we had to find a place of our own, which became very clear when I got pregnant with our son. Mike soon found a full-time job as an Assistant Manager at Pizza Hut. We found a small townhouse apartment and were excited for our baby to be born.

Our son, Nathan, was born on October 21st, 1994. Mike and I had been married for almost three years when he was born, and my mom had not been to visit.

She was very excited about seeing the baby and flew to Texas about a month after Nathan was born. This was the beginning of restoring our relationship since I had moved. She began visiting more often, and I flew up to Massachusetts a few times with Nathan to visit. Unfortunately, Mike had to work, but he was great about letting me visit her.

A few years after the birth of my son, we were both employed full-time. We bought our first house when Nathan was four years old. It was an older home, but it was ours. That made it special for us.

By that time, I had been home to Massachusetts only a few times. I spoke with my siblings periodically over the years. One day, my mom informed me she hadn't spoken with Russ for a few weeks. I called my sister, and she had not heard from him either, which was highly unusual. My mom called the police department in Lynchburg, VA, where he had moved, and filed a missing person report.

A few hours later, in the middle of the night, she got a call that someone had discovered a body in the woods, but it had been there for several weeks and was not identifiable. They told her they would have to check dental records as the face was severely destroyed. They asked if anyone local knew him, and my mom told them the pastor's son from Thomas Road Baptist Church was his good friend.

He was called in to attempt to identify the body. He said it looked like him, but he couldn't be sure because of how bad he looked. They received the dental records back the next day and confirmed it was my brother. We were all devastated and at a loss for what had happened. It was unbelievable!

His property owner informed us that Russ had gone to the psychiatric hospital since his schizophrenia had worsened. We called the hospital, who confirmed and told us that he had checked himself out and left on foot. This sounded exactly like my brother because he did not have a car and walked everywhere.

The police had seen him walking and tried to stop him to ensure he was okay, but he ran. We discovered that he was running through the woods to get to the church and got lost. He fell into the pond and was soaking wet. It was during the winter, and the temperatures were freezing. They determined that he had frozen to death and had been out in the woods for three weeks. Finally, a man and his dog found the body in the woods.

The whole situation was too much to handle. I kept imagining him being out in the cold, freezing to death. I kept hearing his voice asking for help. I couldn't help but wonder what he must've gone through, just how lonely he must have felt in his last moments. The thought of how he died pained me; it devastated all of us.

Russ's body was shipped back to Massachusetts and taken to the funeral home. My dad and his wife, Mike, and I flew home for the funeral. Unfortunately, due to the severity of the decomposition of his body, the funeral director would not allow anyone to view him. In his words, he would not have wanted his own mother to see the body.

It was horrible.

I already had a difficult time dealing with his loss. Not being able to see him and have closure only made it worse. My mind would not allow me to believe he was really gone.

Not only did we have to find some way to handle this loss, my mom and dad had not been in the same room for over 25 years. I was worried about them making a scene or fighting. Thankfully, everyone was too grief-stricken. Moreover, they were both respectful of my brother and were courteous toward each other.

I was glad to leave Massachusetts after the funeral. Mike and I flew back to Texas, and this was when my father started to have a nervous breakdown. He and his wife did not get along, and my father blamed her for not allowing him to be there for my brother. My mother was unsure how to handle his loss either. She tucked her feelings away, not knowing how to deal with this loss.

A few months after my brother died, my father called and told me he was leaving his wife and moving back to New Hampshire. My sister and I were shocked as they had been married for over 25 years. He was so dejected by what had happened to my brother that he could no longer handle staying in his unhappy marriage.

Chapter 8

God's Provision – Renewed Hope

Although I did not get the job I expected to get when I arrived in Texas, God gave me the love of my life. When I started talking to Mike, I knew he would be the one that I would walk down the aisle with. Mike felt the same about me. We rushed to get married rather than waiting for Mike to finish college, but I was so worried he was going to leave me and wanted to make sure we were committed to each other.

God worked through Mike to help me gain the self-confidence I had lacked my entire life. I had been so shy and scared of people, and Mike helped break me out of that shell. Marrying the Wright family showed me a different way of living. Even though I had spent a lot of time with their family being friends with Debbie, being a part of the family through marriage was different. I had to learn how they communicated with a lot of sarcasm. At first, this was difficult since I was so sensitive, but I learned how to handle sarcasm after a while. God realized how strong I would need to be to handle the things coming into our lives.

"God is our refuge and strength, an ever-present help in trouble."

Psalm 46:1a

We consistently moved jobs and apartments during our first several years of marriage. I think I had introduced Mike to the craziness of my childhood. Credit where credit is due, though, for he was always a good sport about it and went along with it, no matter what. God was strengthening us to handle all the curveballs life was throwing our way.

Mike struggled to find a job he liked without a college degree. He worked several part-time jobs while I worked at temporary agencies. Fortunately, God provided Mike with a job that allowed us to return to his hometown of Burkburnett. His family was there to support us. When we first moved back, his parents offered us a place to stay and helped us form a budget to get back on track financially.

"And my God will meet all your needs according to the riches of his glory in Christ Jesus."

Philippians 4:19

I became very depressed and homesick the first few years we were married, and all I wanted was to have a baby. I knew we were not prepared, but I still wanted one. After we moved back to Burkburnett, God allowed me the joy of getting pregnant with our first child. God knew that it was all I needed to get back into the church. Mike and I had not been to church during the first few years of our marriage.

The joy of a newborn son also brought my mom back into my life. She flew to Texas for the first time a month after he was born and loved it. She continued to stay in close contact and came to visit several times. She was such a help to me in learning how to take care of a baby and having someone to talk to through the difficulties we had gone through.

When my brother passed, Mike was my stronghold during the flight and funeral. He was the one person I could let my guard down and be completely myself.

And because he knew how bad the relationship had been between my parents, he was a wonderful distraction. My dad and Mike got along very well, which helped during the intense stress of the situation. God was there at the funeral keeping everyone from getting into fights and blaming one another. This was the first time in 25 years my parents were in the same room, and everything went smoothly.

God continued to protect us on our crazy plane ride home and gave me such a great appreciation for my healthy son and for my family. God was slowly restoring the relationship with my family.

"And the God of all grace, who called you to his eternal glory in Christ, after you have suffered a little while, will himself restore you and make you strong, firm, and steadfast."

I Peter 5:10

Chapter 9

Devastating Loss

The loss of my brother hit me harder than I realized it would. I walked around in a state of disbelief for a long time. I told Mike I desperately wanted another child, but he was unsure if we could afford another child at that time or ever. We began to pray about having another baby for a year, and both had peace about having another child. However, after trying for the next year, I was unable to get pregnant. I went to the doctor, who started me on hormones. A month later, in March 2000, I found out I was pregnant and due in November.

Mike was employed full-time as a guard at the Allred Prison in Wichita Falls, TX. Although the job paid well, he was not happy working in prison; it was a dangerous place to work. He had also been working part-time as a tax preparer for a few tax seasons at H&R Block. I was working for the Clinics of North Texas and had excellent benefits. We were able to catch up on bills, and I was going to be able to stay at home with our children after the birth. Mike had an opportunity for a full-time position with H&R Block as an Assistant District Manager in Arlington, TX. Shortly after the interview, they offered him the job. This was a difficult decision since I liked my OBGYN doctor, and Nathan had just started kindergarten. We agreed that Mike would move to Arlington and start his new position at H&R Block, and I would follow suit, along with the kids, after the school year. Mike would come home every weekend to see Nathan and me.

A few months before our daughter was due, my parents came out to help me. I was so large and miserable; it was all I could do to get through work each day, never mind handling a five-year-old and preparing for a newborn. Finally, my mom and stepdad retired and decided to come to Texas to help me with Nathan and prepare for the baby.

Our daughter Madison was born on November 7, 2000. It was so difficult for Mike only be able to see her on the weekends. With tax season about to begin, it became difficult for him to come home every weekend. He did not feel like he was able to bond with Madison, only seeing her on weekends.

My mom stayed with me after the baby was born, and my stepfather returned home. Although I had her help, I felt Mike's absence and missed him terribly each day. By March 2001, we decided to put our house up for rent and move to Mansfield, a city right outside of Arlington, allowing us to be a whole family again. Shortly after we moved to Mansfield, my mom returned home.

Moving to Mansfield and purchasing a home proved to be a difficult experience since the cost of living was drastically higher in the DFW Metroplex. In addition, our new house flooded a few days after we moved in. Consequently, I ended up having to go back to work, and the stress of the move and Mike's new job working 70+ hours a week was taking a toll on him and our little family.

Over the next few years, I worked at various preschools to be closer to Madison and flexible hours that allowed me to be involved in Nathan's school activities.

Loneliness had always been my friend – and foe. It was something that accompanied me everywhere I went, even though I never welcomed it in my life. It followed me from my childhood to my adulthood. With Mike working so many hours, I felt just like I had when my siblings first moved away, when my grandparents died, or when my mom would go out on dates with men. I felt like a lonely girl on her own. Of course, my relationship with Mike was different and, perhaps, stronger. So, his absence hit me even harder. I felt like a single mom most days.

I know that he worked for us to better our financial situation, so I understood why he wasn't around as much. But not being together as much created a divide and brought a gap between us. We recovered from it, but it took time. Eventually, we were able to work out our differences and put them aside.

Nevertheless, we fell deeper into debt, and the stress piled up.

In 2006, Mike was promoted to District Manager at H&R Block and was busier than ever. We desperately needed the extra income, so I was grateful. However, thanks to the promotion, Mike worked even longer hours, was never home, or had time to spend with the kids or me. We would fight about this and be under constant stress. Fortunately, we were involved in several ministries at our church and had a great group of friends there. Mike was asked to become a deacon at our church in 2007, and life started to ease up.

Mike was in a position where he made a good salary, but his job made him feel miserable. He was depressed because of his work. He couldn't get a better job because he'd left his education midway. He began looking for other jobs in the fall of 2007. However, he could not find anything for which he qualified as he did not have a degree.

After Thanksgiving, I noticed Mike slipping into a deep depression, and I was very concerned. I spoke to him, but he managed to mask his feelings well. We had planned on shopping for Christmas for the kids one weekend in December when we received a call that our credit card had been hacked for over

$900.00. I frantically worked on the budget, trying to figure out what we would do to provide Christmas for the kids. We went out to dinner with some friends on December 14th and had a great time. After dinner, we came home and discussed our plans to go Christmas shopping the next day.

The next morning, we woke up and went about as usual, or so I thought. Mike was moving slowly and was unusually quiet. I was too busy to notice Mike's abnormal behavior. He was the type of person who would get up on Saturday morning and would joke with the kids while cooking breakfast.

A little while after waking up, I was in the office on the computer, trying to figure out our financial situation. He stopped at the door and told me he was going to watch television in the bedroom. I acknowledged but did not really stop to think that he was not feeling well. A little while later, I heard noises coming from the bedroom. I ran in and found Mike sitting in the chair with his eyes rolled back and unresponsive.

I called 9-1-1, and my son came and rushed into the room. While I was screaming and crying, my 13-year-old son stayed calm and assisted me in giving him CPR. Praise the Lord, my seven-year-old daughter was downstairs watching cartoons, unaware of the situation unfolding upstairs.

After administering CPR, for what felt like an eternity, the paramedics showed up and took over. They told me to get dressed and to send my daughter to a neighbor's house. They would not allow me to ride in the ambulance. I had to ride with my neighbor to the hospital. The paramedics called several people for me to inform them what was happening. There were approximately twenty people at the hospital when I arrived.

The nurse led me back to a waiting room, and the doctor came in to inform me, my family, and my friends of the news. I expected to hear that Mike had suffered a heart attack but had stabilized and was resting.

To my shock, the news I received changed my life forever.

"I'm sorry, Ms. Wright, we tried everything to save your husband but were unable to do so. He has died."

This wasn't something I had ever expected – not even in my wildest dreams. I felt my world collapse around me; it was as though I just couldn't breathe anymore. Slowly, I fell to the ground.

Dead? Gone? Mike – my Mike?

He was the love of my life, my soulmate. He was the father of my children. He was my whole world, my past, present, and future. And just like that, with one apologetic sentence, he was gone.

Disbelief washed over me; I could not grasp the news that had been delivered. It felt like a death sentence that took my life and dreams along with it. I tried to come to terms with it, but I just couldn't. The shock eventually wore off, slowly replaced by anguish and misery. I was in so much pain, emotionally and mentally, that I felt dead.

My mom, stepfather, son, and several friends surrounded me, but I felt as though I was alone in a dark hole. I ran to the hospital hallway, praying this was all a bad dream. Everyone talks about dreams coming true with so much positivity. I guess they forget about the bad dreams.

My in-laws were on their way to the hospital and were still an hour away. As I slowly dialed their number, I could barely whisper the words, *"Mike has died."* As I listened to their cries of anguish, my heart hurt deeply. I could barely breathe. All I wanted was to die. The thought of telling my seven-year-old daughter was more than I could bear. As my friend brought her to the hospital, I had to tell her that her daddy was in heaven with Jesus. She immediately asked to see her daddy.

I took my children to see their lifeless father. Our pastor followed us in. As I watched my daughter rub on her daddy's arm and tell him she loved him, I thought I would not make it. My thirteen-year-old son was in shock and was trying to be a man in a boy's body. He grabbed his sister and held her. It was at that moment a piece of me died with Mike.

On December 15, 2007, the trajectory of my life changed forever.

I recall going back to the waiting room where all my friends and family were. I was completely numb and had no idea what to do. My pastor was a lifesaver. He came up to me and explained that he was there for me to guide me through the next steps. I would first have to sign a release to have his body taken to the morgue. I signed the release, not knowing that once I did, no one would be allowed to see him until the funeral. Mike's parents arrived and were terribly upset that they could not see their son. I felt terrible, but I explained that I had no idea.

I vaguely remember the drive back home. My mother, stepfather, in-laws, and kids were there. We sat at the table discussing what had just happened. I felt as though I was in a terrible nightmare and would soon wake up. Only a few hours after Mike died, my in-laws explained I needed to go to the funeral home to make the arrangements. I was not prepared to go to a funeral home. I could not even get over the shock of Mike being gone. I remember them asking me about life insurance. I could not even think straight, let alone think about life insurance. I told them Mike had insurance but was unsure how much.

Upon arriving home from the hospital, I noticed several cars outside my house. My boss had come to the house with food. Several of our friends came to the house to offer their condolences. They wanted me to eat, but I could not. I remember wanting to see my kids and make sure they were okay. Madison was so young that she did not know what was going on, but she enjoyed getting all the attention. Nathan was trying to act like he was okay, but I knew he was not. My heart felt for my two children, but I could not console anyone. As many friends and family approached me, I wanted to be alone. I remember going upstairs to my bedroom and crying. I sat in the dark, trying to figure out what had just happened.

Then, it began. The moment where I blamed myself for not doing CPR correctly, not being a better wife, and not noticing that something was off that morning. I felt like a terrible human being. I should have noticed the signs. I stayed in my room for a long time. People would come in to check on me and try to get me to eat, but I could not. The thought of food made me feel sick.

After the crowd left, and it was only family, the discussion about funeral arrangements happened. My in-laws wanted to go to the funeral home and make preparations. I felt bad because I knew they needed to stay busy and be able to contribute, so I agreed.

The next thing I knew, we were headed to the funeral home. As shock encompassed my body, I was unprepared to plan arrangements for my husband. We were supposed to be going Christmas shopping, not planning a funeral. As I walked into the funeral home, I could barely go in. Funeral homes had always creeped me out as a child, but this was different. This time meant I was saying goodbye to my husband.

The people at the funeral home were wonderful. They understood my shock and emotions. I remember them asking me questions, and I remember just looking at my in-laws and letting them discuss the details. The time came to pick out his casket. I can remember several times during our marriage Mike joking with me, saying, "If I ever die, just put me in a wood box and bury me near the tree in the backyard." Oh, how those words stung me now. I could not bear the thought of him being put in a wooden box. I made sure to pick out a nice casket. As if the funeral home arrangements were not enough, we had to pick a cemetery plot the next day. I felt nauseated and felt as though my head was spinning out of control.

As a 36-year-old, I had no idea what I would do. I was happy that Mike's parents were there to help me make decisions. I was in such a fog and just going through the motions. All I wanted to do was run and get out of there as quickly as possible. It seemed like we were there forever.

After we finally went home, I could not sit still. Jack and Gayle started to settle in, knowing this would take several days, and I told them they could sleep in my room. There was no way I would be able to sleep in our bed.

After we got home, Mike's mom called Mike's work to find out about any life insurance policy he may have had. One of Mike's brothers, Larry, was at the house and asked me how he could contribute. I explained I was afraid of being in the house alone and wanted to have our security system activated. He immediately called the security company and planned to have them come and set up the system. I told everyone I wanted to go to the store. No one would allow me to drive after what I had just gone through, and one of Mike's brothers took me to the store.

I felt the need to return Mike's Christmas gifts since he was gone. I don't know what I was thinking, but I couldn't stay still. I'm sure everyone thought I must have been losing my mind, and honestly, I was. All I could think about was my future, my hope for my kids' future. Everything had stopped. When I got back, it was evening, and I was not hungry, but Mike's parents took over and ensured there was food for everyone.

The rest of the night was a blur, and as I was getting ready to go to bed, I decided I wanted to sleep downstairs on the couch, anywhere but in our bedroom. I laid on the couch all night, crying and praying to God, asking, "why?" I couldn't understand. I wanted him to give me an explanation as to why He would take my husband, my children's dad. Mike was the best person I ever knew. He never did anything to hurt anyone. I could not understand why God had to take him from me. As I lay on the couch, I knew I wouldn't get any sleep that night. I remember having severe anxiety. I finally called my sister at 2 am. She picked up the phone and graciously told me she knew how distraught I was and was unsure how to help.

The following morning, she called me and told me my dad and her were flying out to be with me and be there for the funeral. I remember being happy they were coming but also concerned since my dad and mom weren't on speaking terms, and I could not cope with any problems at the funeral. I told my sister it was okay for my dad to come, but he had to understand that my mom would also be at the house. She said he understood.

On Sunday afternoon, Mike's parents began speaking with me about going to the flower shop to get flowers and going to the cemetery to find a plot on Monday morning. Nathan was standing there listening as we made plans, and I told him he was not expected to join me. He told me he wanted to go to school, and I totally understood. I would have run away if I could have. I planned to send Madison to school the next day to try to keep her busy as well. My mom told me not to worry about Madison. She was happy to watch her for me.

The following day, when we got up, I saw Nathan, who wasn't getting ready to go to school. So, I asked him, "I thought you were going to school today?"

He told me he had changed his mind and wanted to go with us. I wanted to make sure he did not feel obligated. I knew how much this was taking a toll on him and how stressed he was. Nathan bottled up his feelings and never complained; he was just like his dad. Mike's parents thought it might be a good idea to let him come and have some sense of control over an uncontrollable situation.

We went to the florist to pick out a floral arrangement for the casket, and I had no idea what to get. The florist showed me the book and the choices available. Nathan stood up and pointed to an arrangement with white roses and said, "That's the one, mom. Dad's favorite color was white, and those are the ones I want for his casket." I told him we could do whatever he wanted, and I was sure his dad would love them.

After we left the florist, we went to the cemetery closest to the house. As we were driving, I stared out the window, not knowing what to do. I was so distraught thinking about Mike and how I was supposed to be shopping for Christmas. Now, I was riding through a cemetery, trying to find a place to put him to rest. Nathan looked over and saw a tree in the cemetery, and he said, "That's where I want Dad buried. I want him under that tree. It looks so peaceful."

We saw an empty lot, and I told him, "Nathan, if this is where you want your dad to be buried, that's fine with me."

We chose the plot and were done. All that was needed was to find someone to sing at the funeral. I asked two of our friends if they would be willing to sing, and they agreed. I decided I wanted to have the funeral at our church, where Mike had become a deacon that year, the church we had been attending for ten years and invested our lives in, where all of us felt comfortable and safe. Our pastor was going to lead the ceremony. He told me the church ladies were making lunch for the family before the funeral.

The next day my sister and father flew in, and we went to the airport to pick them up. It was nice to have more of my family here, as most of my house was filled with Mike's family. My mom and stepdad were there as my sister and dad arrived. Everyone knew this was such a stressful situation, and humor was the best way to deal with everything.

My dad surprised me. He was good at keeping the peace with my mom and joking around with my stepdad. We decided to have the funeral at the end of the week as we had to wait for out-of-town siblings and family to arrive. Mike's funeral would be only a few short days before Christmas – this was hard to handle. I knew this would be at the forefront of my mind each year at Christmas, and I had no idea how Christmas would ever be normal again for my kids or me.

Mike's family requested we come to their house on Christmas Eve with the kids and my family to celebrate. I had no interest in going. I was not motivated to celebrate Christmas. All I wanted to do was run away. Finally, they insisted that we go to keep a normal pace for the kids, and I finally agreed.

The day arrived to go to Mike's viewing. As I walked into the funeral home, I felt stiff, like I couldn't move. I had no idea how I was going to be able to go into that room and find my husband lying in a casket, lifeless. I was more concerned about how this was going to affect my kids.

How would they react? What was Madison going to do or think?

I told Mike's parents to please go in first. I knew how anxious they were to see him since they hadn't seen him when he died. They were there for quite some time. After they came out, I went in with my children by my side, and we went up to the casket. Madison had insisted that Mike hold a picture she had drawn of him only a few days prior. She wanted her daddy to have that with him when he went to heaven. Seeing him holding a picture she drew made me so emotional. I felt sick.

Madison saw the flowers and immediately went and picked some out of one of the arrangements and put them in her daddy's hands. I immediately began crying. Madison just went around the room, being a little girl with flowers in her hands and just going up and saying hello to people. Nathan was visibly upset, seeing his dad in the casket, and I knew he wanted to get out of the room. He went outside and spent time with his friends just visiting. This was his way of coping with the whole situation.

I'm not sure how many people came to the viewing that night, but I was overwhelmed by how many friends and family came. I felt like I was suffocating as if there was no air in the room to breathe, and with so many people there, I was beginning to get anxious. I wanted to be there with Mike, but I wanted to be elsewhere too. At the end of the night, I recall my friends coming to me asking if there was anything they could do. I told them I would be okay. I went home with my family and tried to prepare myself for the funeral the next day.

In the morning that followed, I knew this was the day I would say my final goodbye to Mike. I was unable to move; all I knew was that I wanted this to be over, but at the same time, I was not ready to say goodbye. I was unsure how I was going to deal with the pain and move on.

After the family meal, the funeral director asked if I wanted to have people come by the casket to pay their final respects. I remember saying no; I was unsure why, but I could not talk to anyone. I asked the funeral director to keep the casket open during the service, which I'm not sure was a good idea, but I wanted to see Mike for as long as possible.

At the end of the service, I remember everyone leaving the sanctuary, allowing Mike's parents, myself, and the kids the opportunity to say our final goodbye. Madison and Nathan went up to the casket, and one of my girlfriends took Madison out. As she was carrying her out of the church, she was halfway down the aisle when Madison yelled, "Wait!" I had no idea what she was doing.

She then explained she needed to kiss her daddy goodbye. We all stood in shock and amazement at this little girl and how strong she was. My friend brought her back down, and she kissed her dad and told him she loved him. Then Madi and Nathan left the church, and Mike's parents said their final goodbyes, leaving me alone with Mike.

I was unsure what to say. I was so scared and hurt I was unsure what to do. I knew it was just me as soon as I walked out of the church, and he was gone. As I left the church, so many people were in the hall, and I wanted to say hello to everyone, but I knew I had to get out of there. Mike's parents, I, and the kids rode in their car to the cemetery right behind the hearse.

Driving to the cemetery seemed to take forever. Once we arrived, I remember thinking, "It's December 20th, and it's warm out." I was angry. It should have been cold and cloudy. That is how I felt inside, as this wasn't a happy time. At the service, my friend sang, "It Is Well with My Soul."

Somehow, God intervened and allowed me to sing. Those words spoke to me and told me He would take care of me. As soon as we left the cemetery and were driving out, I remember having a sense of guilt and relief at the same time. How could I be glad it was over when I had to leave my husband there?

When we returned to the house, Mike's family stayed for a little while and then had to leave since they had a long drive home. They told me they would see me on Christmas Eve. My sister, dad, and parents stayed with me at the house. I still did not know how I was going to sleep in our bedroom. That night I remember Madison wanted to sleep with me, and I allowed her to. I was glad to have her with me.

Chapter 10

God's Provision – A Closer Walk With Jesus

The next few days leading up to Christmas Eve went by quickly, and we went to Plano to celebrate Christmas with Mike's family. I tried to be strong for my kids so they could have a good time. The kids were happy to be around their aunts and uncles and have some normalcy.

The morning that followed was Christmas, and it was all I could do to get out of bed. Christmas had always been my favorite holiday, and I knew I would not ever be able to celebrate the same way again. My father-in-law had taken the kids shopping for gifts, and I cried a lot that morning. Mike and I had bought special gifts for the kids and were excited to see them open on Christmas morning. We had bought Nathan his first drum set, and we got Madison a new swing set. Mike hadn't had the time to put the swing set together, and a few of the men from the church were wonderful enough and came over before Christmas to put it together for her. They were both so excited when I told them their daddy picked out these special gifts for them. We made it through the day, and I was happy to have the holiday over with.

Since I worked for the school district, I had two weeks off for Christmas break, which allowed me to spend a lot of time with the kids and try to get ourselves together before going back to school and working after the new year. Once the holidays were over, one of my brothers-in-law spent a great deal of time helping me with financial matters. I wanted to trade in my old minivan and get a new, more dependable car. I also wanted to make sure to invest the life insurance money Mike left us and ensure we would be okay.

I am so thankful that Mike and I had always done our budget together. We were not the best at saving money and did not have a lot, but we did have dreams and discussed what we wanted to do for the future for the kids and us. I am so thankful Mike always thought of the kids and me. He left us in a good position upon his death to take care of us financially without his salary.

The day came for all of us to go back to school and work. Madison cried and did not want to go. It was tough convincing her to go. On the other hand, I think that Nathan was in denial. All he wanted to do was go to school and try to act like nothing was wrong. I think Nathan wanted to internalize everything, and I believe he felt if he acted like everything was normal, it would be. He did not want anyone to feel sorry for him. Madison, however, seemed happy receiving attention from everyone.

I am so thankful that her teacher was a friend I had worked with at a preschool a few years before. If it hadn't been for her, I don't know if I would have been able to get Madi through the year.

When I returned to work, it was all I could do to make it through the day without being in tears. I was so blessed to have a wonderful boss who understood what I was going through and was very patient with me. I tried reaching out to HR to see if I could take a leave of absence. They strongly discouraged that, and I ended up staying at work.

Over the next few months, I decided to finish the school year and then quit. I knew I needed to stay at home with the kids and try to help them through this challenging transition. I tried to attend as many school functions as I could for the kids, but it was difficult having two kids with activities and only being a single person who couldn't be in two places at once. My parents were wonderful about helping me as much as possible.

I had difficulties feeling like I belonged at church, but I was introduced to a couple at church who helped mentor me through the grief process and checked on me several times a week. The husband had lost his first wife to death early in his marriage after she delivered twins, and he was blessed to meet another wonderful woman about a year later. They were so understanding due to having been through a similar loss and let me speak what was on my mind, no matter how crazy or mad I felt. The biggest thing that stood out to me was them telling me that it was ok to be angry with God for allowing Mike to die. I was told God understands we are human and that we are going to feel anger. It was what we do with those feelings that were important. I spent many lonely nights processing what had happened, crying hysterically and continually asking God *why*. I did not feel like I was getting any answers, and I was alternating between anger, terror, and a feeling like I would have a breakdown.

Madi had been sleeping in my bed since Mike passed away and was afraid to be away from me. She thought if I left her, I might not come back. I felt so bad for her and tried to get her together with her friends as much as possible to get her used to being apart. Nathan wanted to be over with his friends as much as possible. I don't think he knew how to process everything that had happened, and he was in no way prepared to handle my emotions.

A few weeks after going back to school, I received a call from the assistant principal at Nathan's school. He was acting out in class, and they wanted to speak with me. His teachers and the staff knew what had happened and felt sorry for him. I went to talk with the Assistant Principal and worked with the teachers on how to handle his behavior. Nathan and I talked, and I told him that it was okay to be sad and upset about losing his dad. He did not need to act out and try to be the "class clown" to cover his emotions. The school suggested I get him into counseling.

The search for a good counselor for both the kids and me began. I wasn't sure where to start. I had someone refer me to a place in Ft. Worth called "The Warm Place," which offers therapy to families who have been through the loss of a parent, spouse, sibling, etc.

When I called, they advised me we could begin counseling three months after the loss. I wasn't sure why we had to wait, but I would later understand. So, I found a temporary counselor for both Nathan and Madison. Nathan quickly learned that if he said all the right things, the counselor would think he was fine and not ready to get help. Madison had a hard time articulating her feelings since she was so young and could not understand what had happened. I also tried to find a counselor, but everyone I went to did not help.

Over the next few months, as we were waiting to go to The Warm Place, I did my best to manage the kids, the house, and work. I struggled every morning with Madi going to school. It was hard enough for me to motivate myself to go to work. My mom tried to help in every way she could. She was unsure how to help, but I did use her help many times. Nathan eventually got to where he just wanted to hang out with friends from church as often as possible to avoid being in the house. He wanted away from the crying and depressed state of our home.

I was never the family's cook, and we ate out a lot and had simple meals. I felt sorry for the kids since Mike was a great cook. I began to practice cooking things I had never made before and expanded my cooking skills the best I knew how, often with tears streaming down my face, not knowing how I would keep this up.

Mike and I had only lived in the house for a few months before he died. Since it was a new house, we constantly had salespeople coming by the house trying to sell me something.

I remember one evening after dark, the doorbell rang. I was so terrified of being alone that I went and hid in my closet and started crying. I don't know why I was so afraid, but anytime Mike went out of town, I hated being alone. At this point, I knew I had to get to where I was not afraid to be alone. Since Nathan always wanted to go to friends' houses, Madison began to want to as well. This often left me alone in the house, and I had to overcome my fear. I was determined not to be afraid to be alone and to let God work through me to overcome my fear. After a few months of being alone, I looked forward to it. I enjoyed having a break from being the strong one all the time, which gave me time to grieve. I knew I needed to make friends, but I still wasn't ready.

Mike was the computer guru of the family and always handled all the electronic issues in the house. One evening when I was working on the computer, it crashed, and I lost everything. I used Quicken, and all my financials were on that program. I remember sitting in the middle of the office, screaming at Mike. I knew he wasn't there to hear me, but I needed to vent. The kids came by the room and looked at me like I had lost my mind. I felt like I had. At that moment, I realized that I had to begin learning how to take care of myself and my kids alone.

Fortunately, Mike had provided well for us in life insurance, and I was able to pay off our debt and have enough to live comfortably. Unfortunately, I often purchased things for the kids out of guilt and wanting to make them happy. I was unable to realize at the time that all they needed was love and attention.

After the three-month waiting period, we went to "The Warm Place" for our first session. Dinner was provided first, and then small groups after, where we were able to meet others going through similar circumstances. Many of the people in attendance had lost a loved one anywhere from six months to many years prior. It was at that point I realized how much farther along they were in their grief process and had more capacity to handle it. I wanted to make the best of this for myself and the kids, so I kept a positive attitude.

After dinner, the kids were divided by age, and the adults were together in group sessions. They were amazing working with the kids according to what they could handle emotionally and age appropriately. The adult session was overwhelming for me as many were so much further along in dealing with their losses. I soon realized this is why they wanted people to wait.

As we left therapy each week, Madison would break down crying, while Nathan did not want to talk about any of it. A few months into therapy, I decided it was doing more harm than good, and we stopped going. I found a different counselor for Madison, and per Nathan's counselor, he advised it was not the right time for him; he wasn't ready to deal with his grief.

After we stopped therapy, I determined I needed to be home for my kids. I wasn't sure what I was going to do, but Madison barely survived the first grade, and Nathan was struggling internally. I knew they needed me there for them. I told my boss I would work until the end of the school year, and he completely understood. This gave me something to look forward to, as I had always wanted to be home with my kids.

As the end of the school year approached, I decided it would be nice to go to New Hampshire to visit my father, my sister, and my family. I planned a trip, and we were all excited.

I also knew I needed to figure out something for Madison's school issues. I began speaking with friends of mine, and they suggested looking into a small private school that was close by called "Fellowship Academy." Madison and I went to look at the school, and she immediately fell in love.

Only twelve kids were in each class, and they were like a small family. I explained to the second-grade teacher what had happened, and she was wonderful speaking to Madison. I knew that was where she belonged. I was so glad we had a safe place for her to go and feel secure. They had many activities involving parents and a big end-of-the-school-year trip each year that I could attend with her. She was so excited. Nathan had come a long way during the school year and was ready for eighth grade. He loved being in the band as a percussionist and tried several sports.

Summer came, and we went to visit family in New Hampshire. It was nice to have a change of scenery and spend time with my family, whom we did not see often. It was hard staying with my father and stepmother since they were not good with young kids. My dad got agitated a few times, but we made it through. The kids enjoyed going to different places where I grew up as a child and spending time with their other cousins and grandparents.

When we returned home from our trip, I began thinking about what I wanted to do with my life once the kids returned to school. Our church had a preschool program. I thought it would be nice to work part-time to give me something to occupy my time, and I had several years of experience working with children. I spoke with the director of our church, and she had an opening. I agreed to work a few days a week. I knew this would still leave me a lot of open time to be there for the kids' school activities. Mike and I had never gotten our degrees, and I thought it would be a great time to take some college classes and see how it went. The kids thought it was great that I would go to school and do homework with them.

I also knew I needed to find a way to get involved in church again. I met with the pastor's wife and decided to join the women's ministry team. I loved planning events, which would allow me to meet other women in the church. This was helpful as it took my mind off things for a bit. I now had a hectic schedule, and I knew this would help keep my mind busy. Throughout the year, my mentor stayed in contact with me to see how I was managing my first year alone. I continually aimed to be busy so as not to think about the loss, but through the help of my mentors, I realized I needed to deal with the loss and go through the multiple stages of grief. They explained that I would go through many stages of grief and that it was perfectly normal. I do not know how I would have survived had I not had them to lean on through this difficult time. They were my saving grace since I was not able to find a good counselor.

Fall approached quickly, and the kids went back to school. I began working at the preschool and started two college classes. It had been over 15 years since I had stepped foot in a classroom, and I felt extremely out of place in a junior college with a bunch of young kids. I enjoyed teaching in preschool again and met some very nice women who were there for me through the good times and bad.

I loved being at the kids' school activities and became very involved with Madison's class activities. I would also meet her for lunch and go on field trips with her class. I also tried to meet Nathan for lunch, but he preferred I drop him something off and leave; it just wasn't cool having your mom at school in junior high. The kids were doing much better in school, and I was happy to see them enjoying their school and friends. They also began asking to spend the night at friends' houses more. After several times of them going, I began to enjoy my alone time and started making some new friends at church.

About a month into the college semester, I realized I was not ready for school. My mind was still not in a good place after losing Mike, which instilled a fear of being unsuccessful. I went to speak to the counselor, and she completely understood. I knew I wanted to pursue my education, but I also knew I needed more time to heal and prepare my mind. I continued working at the preschool and participating in the kids' school activities.

Later that fall, my mom informed me of a new Sunday school class starting at her church for single adults. I did not feel like I was ready for that, but she believed it was time for me to go out and meet other single people and form a new life for myself. My children began settling into our new life - they were still not recovered emotionally. I knew that would take a long time, but I needed to find a life for myself now that Mike was no longer with me. I decided to go and give it a try. I am thankful that I did, as I met new friends and my future husband. I was not looking for someone, but God had other plans in mind.

Coming close to the first anniversary, I knew I did not want to have Christmas at home. Too many fresh memories of his death. I decided to take the kids on a Disney cruise for Christmas. We were all very excited. Unfortunately, once on the cruise, Madison got sick. It was a long four days until we could return home. Once we returned home, she started feeling better. I was trying to avoid the anniversary of his death, and even though I was away, it still hurt. I had to learn that time Jesus heals all wounds.

I still asked God *"why"* so many times, but I eventually heard a still, small voice tell me, "Kathy, I determine the days of every person's life, and Mike fulfilled what I wanted him to do, and now he is home where he belongs."

"All the days ordained for me were written in your book before one of them came to be."

Psalm 139:16

I learned I had to make peace with loss in my life, and you never get over the loss of someone close to you…you learn to get through it day by day.

Being a widow and raising children alone was not easy. However, once I allowed Jesus to help me each day and develop a closer walk with Him, He continued the healing process. It took many years to reach a point of acceptance, but I now know, without a doubt, that my loved ones are walking the streets of gold with Jesus, and I will join them one day. The loss is not permanent.

It is temporary, as I know they were believers, and so am I.

What Living Through Loss Taught Me

- Life is short. Tell people you love them every day.
- Do not take time for granted; enjoy every second.
- Do not sweat the small stuff; things will get done.
- Let others help you. You don't always have to do everything yourself.
- Do not take work home. Go home and enjoy your family.
- Do not blame yourself for things you did or thought you should have done.
- Make sure to remind yourself that others understand how much you love them even when you say something hurtful.
- Remember the good things and forget the bad.

What Becoming a Widow Taught Me

- Enjoy your marriage. Take time to spend with each other as often as possible.
- Make sure to have someone help you with your finances. This is not a time to stress about money.
- Report the death to the credit bureaus so others cannot assume their identity.
- Cancel your late spouse's driver's license. It provides identity protection as well.
- Take one day at a time. One breath at a time if necessary.
- Take the time to grieve. Do not let others tell you how long you should grieve.
- When you are ready, seek out a grief share group and/or counseling.
- Be there for your kids. They need you now more than ever.
- Understand God still has a purpose for your life. Life will go on, and you must go on as well.

Conclusion

I am finishing this book as I near my 52nd birthday, meaning it has taken me two years to complete. This has been a journey of pain, sadness, healing, and peace.

As I stated, you never get over losing someone, but with God's help, you get through it day by day.

For those who do not think they will ever be able to have a happy, healthy, normal life again, take it from me. You will.

It will take time, and you must understand there are many stages of grief. You will not always go through them in order, either. In addition, you may go through a stage more than once. Allow yourself to grieve, and do not let anyone tell you how long you should grieve. No one can determine that but *you*.

"Peace I leave with you, my peace I give you. I do not give to you as the world gives. Do not let your hearts be troubled, and do not be afraid."

John 14:27

God can bring peace to your past, purpose to your present, and hope to your future.

My purpose in writing this book is to let others know that I have experienced a great amount of loss. But each loss has taught me something different, and each loss has allowed me to develop a closer relationship with Jesus. I pray that you will find a bit of peace, comfort, and hope after reading this book, and please know that I will be in prayer for all those who have or are in the stages of dealing with a loss.

Made in the USA
Columbia, SC
24 April 2025